GW00360155

Frozen with Fear

Janice Pimm • Jon Stuart

Contents

OXFORD

UNIVERSITY PRESS

Macro Marvel
(billionaire inventor)

Welcome to Micro World!

Macro Marvel invented Micro World – a micro-sized theme park where you have to shrink to get in.

A computer called *CODE* controls Micro World and all the robots inside – MITEs and BITEs.

A MITE

A BITE

Disaster strikes!

CODE goes wrong on opening day. CODE wants to shrink the world.

Macro Marvel is trapped inside the park ...

2

Enter Team X!

Four micro agents – **Max, Cat, Ant** and **Tiger** – are sent to rescue Macro Marvel and defeat CODE.

Mini Marvel joins Team X.

Mini Marvel
(Macro's daughter)

Together they have to:

- Defeat the BITEs
- Collect the CODE keys
- Rescue Macro Marvel
- Stop CODE
- Save the world!

**CODE key
(7 collected)**

Look at the map on page 4. You are in the Big Freeze zone.

3

Before you read

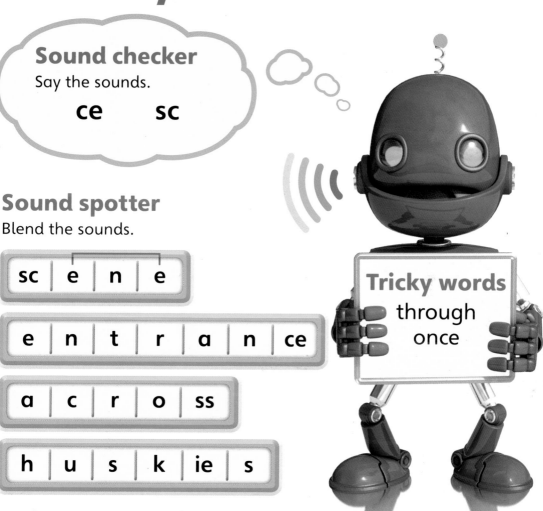

Sound checker

Say the sounds.

ce   sc

Sound spotter

Blend the sounds.

sc	e	n	e

e	n	t	r	a	n	ce

a	c	r	o	ss

h	u	s	k	ie	s

Tricky words

through
once

Into the zone

What do you think the
Big Freeze zone might be like?

5

Big Freeze

Team X, Mini and Rex were at the entrance to Big Freeze. Mini looked at her Gizmo.

Big Freeze

Have fun in Big Freeze.

Enjoy a scenic ride through snow and ice!
Take the Skyway and go high in the air.
Look down at the snowy scene!

You can stop at different places on the way up.

Snow Sports

Race on the toboggans and skate across the ice.

Husky Rides

Let the huskies pull you through the snow.

Snow Dens

Make a snowy house to hide in.

Big Freeze

Have a cool time!

Once you reach the top, swoop downhill at an amazing pace!

Now you have read ...
Big Freeze

Take a closer look
Look back at the text. Can you find words that encourage people to visit this zone?

Thinking time
Imagine you are one of the MITEs on a toboggan. What can you hear, see, smell and touch? How do you feel?

I love snow and ice!

11

Before you read

Sound checker
Say the sounds.

ce   sc

Sound spotter
Blend the sounds.

sc	e	n	t

s	i	l	e	n	ce

d	i	s	t	a	n	ce

Tricky words

once
eyes

Into the zone
What do you think Team X and Mini will do first in this zone?

12

Frozen Footprints

Team X, Mini and Rex were on the Skyway looking at the snowy scene. They got off at Snow Sports.

Snow Sports

"What an amazing place!" cried Tiger.
"Let's chase each other, Rex!"

Mini looked extremely cross. "Tiger, we have to find the CODE key," she said, frowning.

Tiger noticed Rex sniffing the snow. "Rex has picked up a scent!" said Tiger. "Look! He's found some big footprints! They could be the BITE's."

Tiger, Mini and Rex set off at once to track the footprints. "I wonder how far away the BITE might be," said Mini. "I hope it's not too close!" replied Tiger.

Suddenly, Rex looked into the distance. His eyes grew wide. It was the BITE!

Snorp!

The BITE was striding down the mountain.
"Oh no!" said Tiger. "It looks fierce and it's coming this way fast!"

The BITE came closer and closer. "Quick! Let's shrink!" cried Mini.

Tiger, Mini and Rex hid in silence. The BITE's big foot nearly trod on them!

The BITE stopped. It sensed something but it didn't see anyone. It stomped off.

"This is the scariest BITE so far!" whispered Mini.

"I know. The BITE missed us this time but I'm sure we'll see it again," said Tiger.

23

Now you have read ...
Frozen Footprints

Take a closer look
How did Rex use his nose and eyes
to help find the BITE?

Thinking time
What do you think Tiger and Mini would
say about this zone?

I like the Big Freeze
zone because ...

I don't like the Big Freeze
zone because ...